MY DOG IS A HERO

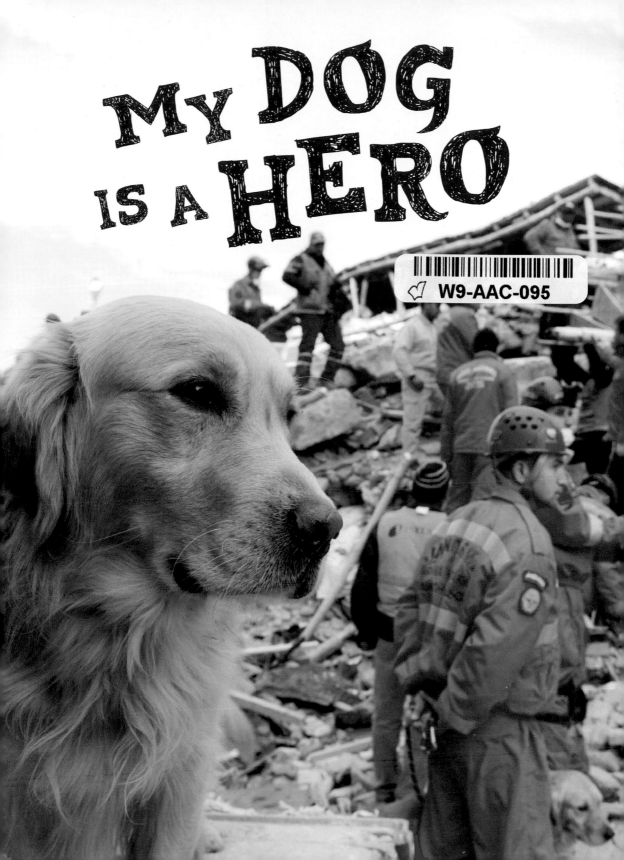

MY DOG IS A HERO

Anita Ganeri

Scholastic Inc.

Conceived, edited, and designed by Marshall Editions
A Quarto Group company
The Old Brewery
6 Blundell Street
London N7 9BH

ISBN 978-0-545-49595-0

12 11 10 9 8 7 6 5 4 3 2 1   12 13 14 15 16 17/0

Printed and bound in China
First Scholastic edition, November 2012

Editor: Carey Scott
Designer: Dave Ball

CONTENTS

INTRODUCTION

Dogs are known as man's best friend, but they can be much more than friends to humans. Every day, dogs carry out heroic acts for us, from serving those in need to lifesaving feats.

As well as learning to detect drugs and explosives, the dogs at this police dog training school in Colombia also train for dog shows.

MEET THE TEAM

Most of the dogs you will read about in this book have human handlers who control them when they are working. The dog and handler rely on each other, working as a team.

HEROIC DOG AWARDS

Each year many heroic dogs—and sometimes their handlers—are awarded medals for their heroic acts. An example of this award is the National Hero Dog Award.

HEROIC DOGS
+ Save lives by helping rescue people from danger
+ Work with the police as detection dogs
+ Help people with physical disabilities
+ Work with soldiers in combat zones

A sniffer dog and handler investigate a case of suspected arson.

In this training session, a water rescue dog jumps from a hovering helicopter to help a struggling swimmer.

1 Lifesavers

Dogs are invaluable members of emergency services. They can locate trapped people at disaster zones, find the lost and injured in remote places, and even rescue people who are drowning.

LIFESAVER DOGS

Saving lives is the most important job a dog can do! Lifesaver dogs are generally called search-and-rescue (SAR) dogs. They work in both urban (city) and rural (country) places.

A SAR dog searching a collapsed building for trapped people.

Sniffing Skills

A fantastic sense of smell is a dog's main tool for finding injured people. Dogs sniff the air—called air scenting—and the ground—called tracking—to find a human scent.

TOP BREEDS

All sorts of breeds of dog are good at search-and-rescue jobs, but working dogs are often used because of their keen sniffing ability and their strength. Popular SAR dogs include Golden Retrievers, Labradors, Collies, and German Shepherds.

Large brain

Sensitive nose

Strong muscles

Border Collies' high intelligence makes them excellent SAR dogs.

URBAN SAR DOGS

Urban search-and-rescue (USAR) teams look for people trapped in collapsed buildings, usually after natural disasters such as earthquakes, hurricanes, and tsunamis.

USAR dog Baxter searches for survivors in a small space in a building's rubble after the Haiti earthquake of 2010.

Why Use Dogs?

With their brilliant sense of smell, dogs can detect the scent from survivors deep under rubble. They can also squeeze into tight spaces where humans can't fit. Dogs can search just as well in the night, and they can search more quickly than humans.

WHERE THEY WORK

USAR dogs work mainly with fire departments and fire services. Many are members of disaster response teams that travel to different countries. They operate mainly in towns and cities, where large, multistory buildings have collapsed.

This German Shepherd is practicing climbing for entering burning buildings. This is called agility training.

DANGERS FOR DOGS

+ Unstable collapsed buildings
+ Unseen drops
+ Sharp materials, such as glass and concrete
+ Risk of fire from pockets of leaking gas from gas mains
+ Flooded basements

DOG CAMERAS

A system called PAWS (portable all-terrain wireless system) is one of the latest gadgets for SAR dogs. A lightweight video camera that fits onto the dog's head sends images wirelessly to its handler. The handler can see what the dog is looking at in the rubble, and rescuers can talk to and reassure people trapped in a collapsed building.

This Collie is demonstrating the fantastic PAWS system.

INTERNATIONAL EFFORTS

The UK operates a team called International Search and Rescue (ISAR). When a major natural disaster strikes, ISAR speeds to the scene. In the past, ISAR dogs have saved the lives of trapped people after devastating earthquakes in Pakistan, Haiti, and Japan.

A Dalmatian aboard a fire truck, during a parade.

FIREHOUSE DOGS

Many fire stations in the US have mascot dogs who live with the firefighters. The most popular breed of fire station dog is the Dalmatian. In the days when fire engines were horse-drawn carts, Dalmatians ran with the horses, encouraging them to go faster, and leading the way to fires.

SEARCH DOGS ON 9/11

On September 11, 2001, terrorists flew planes into the two towers of the World Trade Center in New York. Both towers collapsed, killing and trapping thousands of people. Nearly 100 USAR dogs helped to look for survivors, sniffing through metal, concrete, and dust.

9/11 hero dog Trakr with owner James Symington in Los Angeles in 2005.

Heroic Award

German Shepherd Trakr found the very last person to be pulled out alive from the rubble. Two days later, Trakr collapsed from exhaustion. He later recovered, and in 2005, the United Nations presented Trakr and his handler, James, with the Extraordinary Service to Humanity Award.

MOUNTAIN AND WILDERNESS RESCUE DOGS

SAR dogs help to look for missing walkers and climbers, who may be lost or lying injured in remote places. They sometimes work with the police to find ill or lost people.

Sniffing Distance . . .

A dog can sniff out a human scent from over 500 yards away (as long as the wind is not blowing too strongly). In this way, SAR dogs can sniff out people that are hidden—in a ditch, cave, or under snow. This means that people are found much sooner when dogs are part of a rescue team. In remote areas, speed saves lives.

HANDLER SKILLS

As well as controlling a dog, a mountain rescue handler needs these skills:

+ Ability to navigate accurately in the wilderness

+ Emergency first aid

+ Physical fitness for long days in the wilderness

+ Climbing skills such as rope work

+ Ability to handle a stretcher on steep ground

In a remote part of the UK, a SAR team is dropped off by a helicopter to search for injured hikers.

AVALANCHE DANGER

An avalanche is a landslide of snow that hurtles down a mountainside at tremendous speed. Anyone hit by an avalanche can end up trapped under snow, unable to move or breathe. Finding people fast is vital—90 percent of people found within 15 minutes survive, but only 30 percent survive for more than 30 minutes.

A victim search training session in the French Alps. Fast searches are vital for success, so dogs must be highly trained.

AVALANCHE RESCUE DOGS

Avalanche rescue dogs move across the snow, sniffing for human scent. Dogs can sniff out people buried up to about four yards under the surface. A dog can search an area of snow the size of a soccer field in about 15 minutes. It would take a human nearly two days to search the same area using avalanche poles.

THE FAMOUS ST. BERNARD

The St. Bernard is a breed of dog famous for rescuing people in the Alps. In fact, the legendary St. Bernard was the very first SAR dog! In 980 A.D., a monk named Bernard built a monastery and a hostel in a mountain pass named the Great St. Bernard Pass between Switzerland and Italy. Pilgrims and travelers often got lost or trapped in the snow, and the monks went out to rescue them.

St. Bernards are said to have saved more than 2,000 lives over the centuries.

Very thick fur keeps dog warm in snow

The Great St. Bernard Pass, with its monastery and hostel.

Dogs to the Rescue

Then, the monks began taking the monastery's guard dogs on rescue missions with them. The dogs sniffed out missing travelers, and licked their faces! They could even guide the monks home in the thick snow.

Barry the St. Bernard

A great St. Bernard dog named Barry lived at the monastery between 1800 and 1812. He is famous for saving the lives of more than 40 people, many of them children.

WATER RESCUE DOGS

All dogs can swim naturally, but some breeds are particularly strong swimmers. They can be trained as water rescue dogs, helping lifeguards to rescue people in danger in the water.

A Labrador learns to help a lifeguard rescue a person who is drowning.

Leaping In

A water rescue dog might leap into the water from the shore, from a boat, or even from a helicopter. The dog then swims to the person in trouble, lets him or her hang on to a life belt, and swims back to shore or a boat. The dogs normally wear life jackets for their own safety.

Double-layered coat keeps the dog warm in cold water

TOP BREEDS

Popular water rescue breeds include German and Belgian Shepherds and Labrador Retrievers. But the top water rescue breed is the Newfoundland—known as the "Newfy." No other dog is better suited for the water.

Swansea Jack

A Retriever called Swansea Jack was a famous water rescue dog from Wales, UK. Despite not being professionally trained, Swansea Jack would regularly jump into the river to pull people to safety. In total, he saved an incredible 27 lives.

Newfoundlands were first bred as working dogs for fishermen in Newfoundland, Canada.

Rudder-like tail for power and steering

Webbed feet for swimming

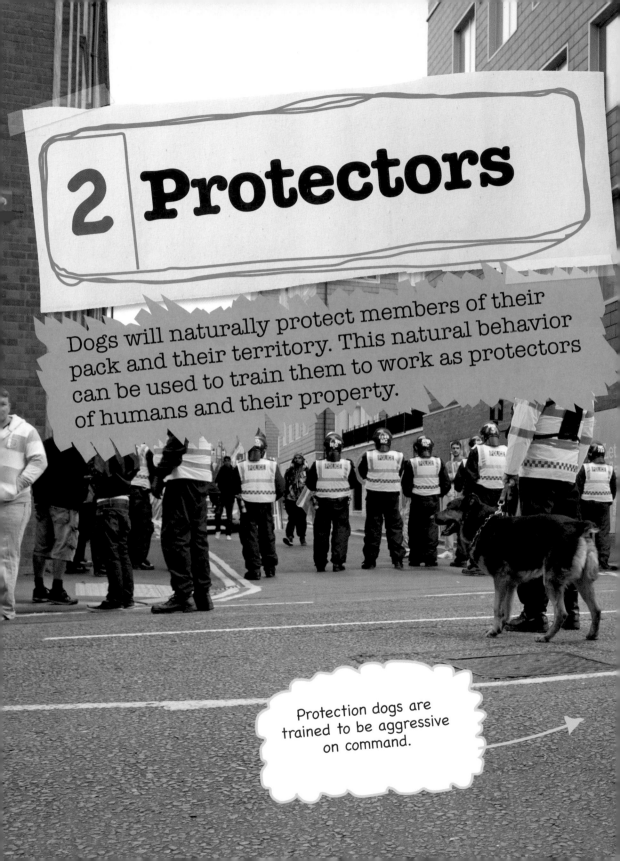

2 Protectors

Dogs will naturally protect members of their pack and their territory. This natural behavior can be used to train them to work as protectors of humans and their property.

Protection dogs are trained to be aggressive on command.

PROTECTORS

Protection dogs work for the police, the military, prisons, private security firms, and private citizens. Protection dogs are almost always big, powerful breeds.

A fierce-looking protection dog, working for a security service, on patrol with its handler.

K-9s

In many countries, protection dogs are known as K-9s or K9s, because it sounds like the scientific name for dog—"canine." Dog handlers are called K-9 handlers, and dog and handler teams are called K-9 units.

TOP BREEDS

As well as being strong, protection dogs must also be courageous and fearless. The most common breed used is the German Shepherd. Other protection dogs include:

- Belgian Malinois
- Rottweilers
- Doberman Pinschers
- American Pit Bull Terriers
- Giant Schnauzers

A male German Shepherd can weigh up to 88 pounds

Strong jaw for holding

Powerful muscles for running and jumping

The first German Shepherds were bred from herding and farm dogs in Germany around 150 years ago.

POLICE PATROL DOGS

Working alongside police officers, dogs can tackle jobs that would be dangerous or impossible for the officers. They can attack armed criminals or chase down suspects.

Police dogs keep unruly fans under control during a soccer game in the UK in 2009. They also protect the officers.

PATROL DOG JOBS

+ Crowd management—at demonstrations, sports events, or VIP events

+ Keeping order, such as during riots

+ Chasing and holding suspects until police officers arrive

+ Tackling armed suspects

+ Searching buildings and open ground for suspects

+ Tracking and sniffing out drugs or explosives

HOLDING SUSPECTS

A dog has two ways of holding onto a suspect—called bark and hold, and bite and hold. In a bark and hold, the dog barks at the suspect, who will normally be scared and stay still. In a bite and hold, the dog bites the suspect and does not let go until its handler tells it to do so.

The most dangerous job that a police patrol dog can do is called firearms support—tackling armed suspects or criminals. Firearms support dogs and their handlers always wear bulletproof vests to protect themselves.

Handler Phil makes sure Obi gets plenty of rest and relaxation during his well-earned break.

The Story of Obi

In 2011, many police dogs and their handlers were sent to help control the crowds during riots in London. One of them, a German Shepherd called Obi, was hit on the head by an object thrown by rioters. Obi suffered a fractured skull. A vet treated Obi, but he couldn't work for several weeks.

MY DOG IS A HERO

"To see your best friend and work colleague get injured while at work is difficult but he is getting a lot of support from everyone. . . ."

PHIL WELLS, HANDLER OF OBI
METROPOLITAN POLICE

POLICE DOG HANDLERS

When they are off duty, police dogs live with their handlers and their families. The dogs have to be sociable and gentle with children, as well as sometimes aggressive when they are on duty. The handler uses signals to tell the dog when it is time to work, or time to play.

Explosives sniffer dog Bertie enjoys playtime with his police officer handler.

New York K-9 officer Bosco shows off his badge.

DOG OFFICERS

In some police forces around the world, police dogs are actually police officers! They are sworn in at a ceremony just like human officers. They get their own identity cards and badges to wear.

Police Dog History

As far as we know, police dogs were first used in 1899, in Belgium, when dogs accompanied police officers on night patrols in the city of Ghent.

SECURITY DOGS

Dogs protect their packs and their territories, so they make good guards. They are used to protect military bases, government sites, factories, building sites, and country borders.

BEWARE GUARD DOG

Most people will stay away from an area if they see a sign like this one! Some security dogs are trained to attack unfamiliar people.

ON PATROL

Most security dogs work with a handler. The dog-and-handler team walks around the site, watching and listening for signs of intruders. Some security dogs work without a handler. They roam free on a site, and are trained to attack any intruder that enters it.

Security dogs must have good eyesight, hearing, and sense of smell to detect intruders or hidden people from a distance.

Clearing an Area

Security dogs and handlers sometimes search sports stadiums, offices, airports, and ships to make sure that nobody suspicious is hiding inside. They check areas one section at a time, and then mark each one to show they are clear.

COMBAT DOGS

Military working dogs, or combat dogs, work with armies, navies, and air forces. A few have a very special role—going on patrol with soldiers, defending them, and taking part in raids.

Combat dog Coot with his US Marine handler on duty in Afghanistan.

MY DOG IS A HERO

"We expect so much of them [the dogs] that we need them to be strong and athletic. We want a highly strung dog with aggressive tendencies because that's what the mission demands."

US ARMY COLONEL DAVID ROLFE

COMBAT DOG JOBS

+ Scouting with foot patrols
+ Helping to clear buildings of enemy combatants
+ Deterring the enemy from attacking soldiers
+ Protecting their handlers
+ Attacking enemy combatants

K-9 EQUIPMENT

Combat dogs have their own special equipment. A flak jacket protects their bodies from bullets and explosions. "Doggles" protect their eyes, and gas masks protect against gas attack. Dogs that go on raids also carry communications equipment.

A police officer fits his dog with a flak jacket, or bulletproof vest, before going on a dangerous mission.

PERSONAL PROTECTORS

Some people keep dogs as protectors as well as family pets. These dogs are known as personal protection dogs or home protection dogs, K-9 bodyguards, and even "24/7 security with fur!"

A young girl cuddles up with her personal protector—a brindle Greyhound.

TRAINING AND BREEDING

Most personal protection dogs are trained by private companies, and owners buy the ready-trained dogs. They must be large, powerful, brave, bold, and confident dogs. The Doberman Pinscher is a popular choice.

The first Doberman was bred in 1890s Germany by a tax collector to protect him on his rounds.

Protectors at Work

Properly trained personal protection dogs are normally friendly. In the street, they stay close to their owners, don't bark or growl, and allow strangers to pet them. But if a dog thinks a person is threatening its owner, it will bark at the person. If the person keeps coming, the dog may become aggressive.

Intelligent and alert

Muscular body

Long legs

HEROIC PET DOGS

Ordinary family dogs sometimes perform extraordinary acts—risking their own lives to protect members of their human families. Some have suffered serious injuries in the process.

BEAR

Debbie Zeisler might have died after suffering a seizure and losing consciousness in her front yard but for the quick action of her dog, Bear. He frantically scratched on every front door in their neighborhood. An animal control officer spotted him and Bear led him to Debbie.

German Shepherd Bear was honored with the 30th National Hero Dog Award in Los Angeles after saving his owner, Debbie.

DIAMOND

This Pitbull woke her owner to alert him to a fire raging through the family's apartment. Then, when 16-year-old Sierra was trapped, Diamond shielded her beneath a mattress until firefightes came to the rescue. She too received a National Hero Dog Award.

After the fire, Diamond spent six weeks at a veterinary hospital recovering from burns and smoke inhalation.

A guide, or Seeing Eye, dog helps a visually impaired man to walk down steps safely.

3 Helper Dogs

Humans can teach dogs to help them in lots of practical ways, but dogs can use their super sense—their incredible smelling ability—to help us in some unexpected ways, too!

HELPER DOGS

Some dogs are trained to help people who have lost their sight or hearing, or who have certain disabilities. They are often called guide dogs. Other helper dogs do jobs such as cattle herding.

If a guide dog sees a car coming too close, it will stop or try to move its owner out of the way.

Helpers and Companions

Guide dogs help people through the streets, listen for sounds, and fetch and carry objects. The dogs are also pets for their owners when they are "off duty."

A baby pets a specially trained "therapy dog" at a children's hospital.

PAT DOGS

PAT stands for Pets as Therapy. PAT dogs visit hospitals, hospices, and nursing homes, where the patients can pet them and talk to them. This helps the patients feel a little better, especially if they are pet owners who cannot have their own pets with them.

HELPER DOG JOBS

✚ Guide dogs help blind or visually impaired people find their way

✚ Hearing dogs act as the ears of a deaf person

✚ Assistance dogs do jobs for people with disabilities

✚ Medical alert dogs signal when a person is falling ill

✚ Herding dogs help farmers to control livestock

GUIDE DOGS

Guide dogs—called Seeing Eye dogs in some countries—help people who are blind or visually impaired. They help their owners walk around safely.

A guide dog helps its owner avoid obstacles while boarding a train.

Meeting a Guide Dog

Many people are tempted to stroke or pet a guide dog if they meet one in the street. But you should not do this without asking its owner. Remember that the dog is doing an important job, and should not be distracted!

High intelligence means trainability

WHEN YOU MEET A PERSON WITH A GUIDE DOG...

✗ Don't ignore the owner and only talk to the dog!

✗ Don't give a guide dog food

✗ Don't pet or stroke a guide dog unless its owner says it's okay to do so

✓ Do offer to help the person cross the road.

Loyal, loving nature

MY DOG IS A HERO

"I'm in and out now on walks all the time—meeting friends, going to the park, and into the city shops. I wouldn't have had the confidence to do all this before."

ANDREA COOPER, GUIDE DOG OWNER

TOP BREEDS

Guide dogs are chosen for their calm temperament and ability to be trained for such a special job. The most popular breeds are Golden Retrievers, Labradors, and German Shepherds.

A Labrador Retriever makes an excellent guide dog.

GUIDE DOG TRAINING

In most countries, guide dogs are given to blind or visually impaired people by charities—Guiding Eyes for the Blind in the US. The charities normally breed and train the dogs, too, and hand over fully trained dogs to their new owners.

Raising Puppies

When the puppies are about two months old, they go to live with people called puppy raisers. The puppy raisers give the puppies obedience training, and get them used to people and other dogs, and to the sights and sounds of the streets.

These puppy trainees wear clearly labeled coats, so passersby can see they have important work to do!

Street Training

When the puppies are about a year old, they leave their puppy raisers and spend up to six months learning to be guide dogs. They practice guiding their trainers along streets, across roads, in and out of shops and restaurants, and on and off of buses and trains.

With a blindfolded trainer, a young Labrador learns how to negotiate hazards.

HEARING DOGS

Hearing dogs work as the ears of their deaf or hearing-impaired owners. They are trained to alert their owners when they hear the doorbell, phone, and other important sounds.

This hearing dog, a tiny Chihuahua, listens intently for any sounds of danger.

Everyday Sounds . . .

Hearing dogs listen for everyday sounds, inside and outside the home. The dog alerts its owner to a sound by touching with a paw or nudging with its nose. Then it takes the owner to the source of the sound.

... and Danger Signals

Dogs also listen for danger signals, such as smoke alarms. If a dog hears an alarm, it gives its owner an emergency alert, such as lying on the ground.

TOP BREEDS

Popular breeds for hearing dogs are Labradors, Golden Retrievers, Cocker Spaniels, miniature Poodles, and King Charles Spaniels.

The King Charles Spaniel is both confident and adaptable.

ASSISTANCE DOGS

Mobility assistance dogs can be a great help to people with physical disabilities, who have lost mobility in a part of their bodies, or who have lost a limb because of accident or illness.

Assistance dog Blaze practices retrieving a phone. Blaze is training to be an Iraqi war veteran's dog.

ASSISTANCE TRAINING

Royal Navy Officer Allen Parton was paralyzed by a head injury while serving in the Gulf War. After five years in hospitals, assistance dog Endal completely changed his life. In 2010, Allen started a UK charity called Hounds for Heroes, to train assistance dogs to help other injured servicemen.

A diabetic teen shops for shoes with his trusty alert dog, Snap. Alert dogs go everywhere with their owners.

DIABETIC ALERT

Most medical alert dogs work with people who are suffering from a disease called diabetes. People with diabetes can develop a dangerous condition called hypoglycemia, which makes them collapse and become unconscious. Amazingly, a trained dog, called a hypo alert dog, can tell if this is about to happen, and alert its owner.

MY DOG IS A HERO

"Scrabble automatically picks up that when I'm in a certain way I show certain behaviors. He seems to pick something up from my breath when I start to go into a hypoglycemic state and he warns me."

PETE, ASSISTANCE DOG OWNER

HERDING DOGS

Dogs help farmers all over the world by herding livestock—mainly cattle and sheep, but also goats, reindeer, and even ducks! They are called herding dogs, stock dogs, or working dogs.

In Australia, sheep are kept on huge ranches called sheep stations.

MAKING MOVES

Cattle herding dogs make cattle move by nipping them on the heels, or by barking at them. Herding dogs often work as a team to control a big herd or flock. Some dogs drive the livestock along, and others steer the livestock from side to side.

TOP BREEDS

Dozens of breeds of dog are workers. Here are a few breeds from around the world:

- Australian Cattle Dog – Australia
- Kelpie – Australia
- Border Collie – UK
- English Shepherd – US
- Welsh Sheepdog – UK
- Lapphund – Scandinavia

This Red Heeler is a type of Australian Cattle Dog.

CONTROLLING HERD DOGS

Farmers and shepherds command their dogs by voice, whistles, and hand movements. Here are some example voice commands:

- **come-bye:** go the left
- **away:** go to the right
- **steady:** slow down
- **stand / wait:** stop
- **cast:** gather animals into a group
- **that'll do:** stop working

4 | Detectors

All over the world, humans utilize dogs' incredible sense of smell to detect both people and things—from explosive devices and criminals on the run to diseases inside our bodies.

Springer Spaniel Toby, an explosive sniffer dog, arrives in Helmand, Afghanistan, to assist a team of British soldiers.

DETECTORS

With their amazingly powerful sense of smell, dogs can be trained to sniff out explosives, illegal drugs, and criminal suspects. These dogs are known as detection dogs, or "sniffer" dogs.

TOP BREEDS

Some dog breeds have more sensitive noses than others. Talented sniffers include sporting breeds, such as Spaniels, Retrievers, and Vizslas, and some working dogs, such as German Shepherds.

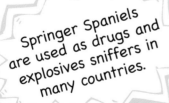

Springer Spaniels are used as drugs and explosives sniffers in many countries.

AN AMAZING SENSE OF SMELL

Dogs have about 200 million smell receptor cells inside their noses—40 times as many as you. They also have an organ in their mouth that allows them to taste the air—like an extra nose. With these two abilities, dogs can sniff out just one scent from a mixture of many.

A dog's nose is its most important sense organ. It uses smell to interpret the world, as humans do with their vision.

SNIFFER DOG TRAINING

Substances such as illegal drugs and explosives give off a scent, and it is this particular scent that sniffer dogs are trained to detect. They are also trained to give their handlers a signal, called an alert, when they find what they are looking for.

These adorable Spaniel puppies have been selected by a specialist sniffer dog training company in Pretoria, South Africa.

Puppies for Training

Most sniffer dogs are bred specially for sniffer dog training. Others come from dog rescue centers. Puppies take an aptitude test before joining a training program. Training starts when the puppies are just a few months old.

A young Labrador sniffs a jar during scent training. When it finds a substance, its handler rewards it with snacks and praise.

Learning a Scent

To train a dog to recognize the scent of a substance, several containers are put on the ground. Only some of them contain the substance. When the dog sniffs one containing the substance, it gets a reward. To the dog, it is a fun game.

EXPLOSIVE DETECTORS

Explosive detection dogs work with the police, customs officers, and armed services, helping to fight crime, terrorism, and enemy forces. They help to keep people safe from bombs and guns.

German Shepherd Ali inspects a suspicious vehicle at the US–Mexico border.

EXPLOSIVE TYPES

Explosive detection dogs search for high explosives—used to create the explosions in bombs and missiles—and explosives called propellants, which are used in firearms. They can detect even the smallest traces, including the residues, of explosives.

Bomb-sniffing expert Spencer on a routine patrol at Detroit Metropolitan Airport, Michigan in 2009.

MILITARY BOMB DOGS

Explosive detection dogs (sometimes called EDDs) work with armed forces. Being an EDD is probably the most dangerous job a dog can do! Most dangerous of all is searching for hidden roadside bombs. They also help troops search for enemy bombs, weapons, and ammunition, helping to save both troops and civilians from attack and injury.

MY DOG IS A HERO

"Treo truly is a wonder dog. Without his work in Afghanistan, there is no doubt soldiers would have suffered serious injuries and could have died if the IEDs [improvised explosive devices] had exploded."

SERGEANT DAVE HEYHOE, BRITISH ARMY

Forming a Friendship

EDD dogs and their handlers form a strong bond when they train and work together. They rely on each other to stay safe. The handlers look after the dogs when the team is off duty, keeping them healthy and playing with them.

In 2010, a black Labrador called Treo was awarded the Dickin Medal, the UK's top military animal bravery award. Treo received the medal for finding two huge roadside bombs while patrolling in Afghanistan.

On a tour of Afghanistan in 2010, explosive detection dog Tinus sniffed out two large mortars—types of bombs—hidden in an abandoned house. The deadly weapons were then made safe by explosive experts. Tinus's expert sniffing probably saved the lives of many soldiers and civilians.

Bomb-sniffing black Labrador Goodwin at work in Afghanistan. He and his human team are digging for a suspected bomb.

Combat Zone Vets

EDD dogs sometimes get injured, and they sometimes just get sick. There are always military vets in combat zones to treat the dogs' injuries and illnesses.

TOP MILITARY DOG AWARDS

UK:
PDSA Dickin Medal

US:
American Humane Association Hero Dog Award

Australia:
War Dog Operational Medal

DRUG DETECTORS

The job of a drug detection dog—or a narcotic detector canine—is to sniff out illegal drugs. They could be in people's clothes, bags, vehicles, or even buried underground.

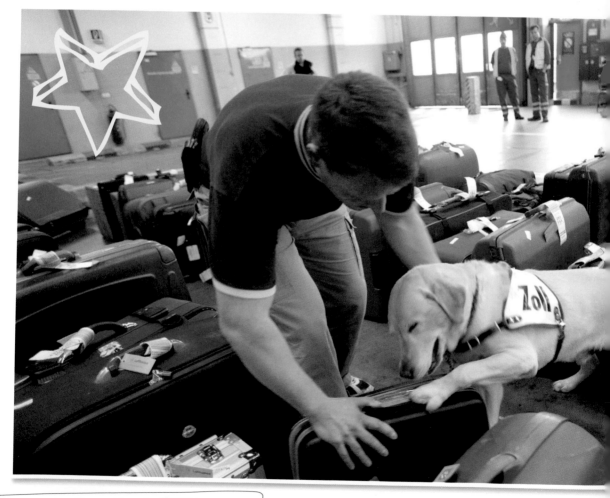

WHERE DRUG DETECTORS WORK

Drug detection dogs work for the police, for customs services, and sometimes for private organizations.

This Spaniel drug detector searches bags on the conveyor belt at an airport.

At the customs hall at Frankfurt airport in Germany, a detection dog searches luggage for illegal drugs.

Border Searches

Drug detection dogs sniff passengers and their baggage as they pass through the security gates at airports, seaports, and at the borders between countries. If a dog detects drugs on a person, customs officers stop and search him or her.

Narrow head

Excellent sense of smell

Pointers are tall and can detect scents from people's upper bodies, making them good passive searchers.

Long legs

TIME TO SEARCH

Dogs carry out two types of searches. Passive searches are sniffing people walking through public areas, such as airports. Proactive searches are used to search a particular person, bag, or area, if officials suspect there could be drugs hidden there.

Pointers are popular drug detection dogs

TOP BREEDS

Pointers indicate things they find by standing rigid and pointing with their bodies, which is why they are called pointers. This habit, along with their keen noses and their height, makes them excellent searching dogs.

A canine officer and his dog, Hex, search for illegal drugs aboard a cargo vessel at Long Beach, California.

Sniffing the Air

Locked containers are hard to search, so handlers set up a machine that pumps air out of the container and blows it through a filter, which traps scents. The dogs sniff the filter to check for drugs. This is called remote air sampling, or vapor extraction.

FINDING PEOPLE

You might not be able to smell the scents of the people around you, but a mantrailing, or "tracker," dog, easily could. These supersniffers can even follow scents across rivers.

This suspect may be able to outrun the police officers, but the tracker dog won't let him get away!

Tracker Targets

Most mantrailing dogs work for the police. They search for suspects who are on the run from the law, escaped prisoners, and people who are missing, perhaps because of illness or injury.

WHAT DOGS SMELL

Sweat contains millions of particles of chemicals that pass into the air, and are carried along in the breeze. These make up a scent, and every person's is unique to them—like a fingerprint. Also, tiny specks of skin are always falling off our bodies, leaving a trail behind us. These also give off a scent that a dog can detect.

This human skin cell, in dust, has been enlarged many times so we can see it. A dog can sniff out these tiny particles.

Once a tracker dog is on your tail, it is very hard to escape! The dogs use two skills to follow you, called scenting and tracking. They can combine the two skills—called trailing—to follow your every move. The dogs work both alone and led by their handlers, and sometimes in small packs.

Once they have identified a scent, tracker dogs just follow their noses.

Here, a Bloodhound takes a good sniff. A suspect's item of clothing can lead a clever tracker dog directly to him or her.

HOW NOT TO ESCAPE

These methods of throwing a mantrailing dog off the scent have all been tried and failed.

✖ Running in a zigzag

✖ Climbing a tree (however tall)

✖ Crossing a river (the dog will pick up your scent on the other side)

✖ Scattering pepper behind you

✖ Washing your clothes

✖ Changing your clothes

Using Skills

A tracker dog can use its scenting skill if it can sniff an item that the suspect has touched, or go to a place the suspect has been. Then it uses its tracking skill to follow the suspect's path. Finally, the dog uses air scenting to home in on the suspect.

BLOODHOUNDS

The Bloodhound has the sharpest nose of any dog breed, and is the best mantrailing dog by a long shot. It is three times better at recognizing scents than any other breed of dog, and can pick out one scent from a mixture of thousands.

Droopy, bloodshot eyes

Extra-sensitive nose

Bloodhounds were originally bred in seventh-century Belgium, for hunting large animals.

Large feet

A Bloodhound and its handlers at Virunga National Park, in the Democratic Republic of Congo, Africa.

National Park Hounds

Staff at some national parks in Africa are creating their own mantrailing programs. They are using Bloodhounds to find and catch illegal hunters, and to locate lost or injured park rangers.

MY DOG IS A HERO

"I'm just still, after all these years, impressed with what they can do. And I still don't know how they do it."

MARLENE ZÄHNER, CONGOHOUNDS

MORE DETECTING DOGS

You have read about dogs that can sniff out drugs, explosives, and people. But sniffer dogs are also trained to search for other things—from cancerous tumors to dead bodies!

A search team with a detection dog tries to locate the bodies of three missing people at the Inner Harbor in Baltimore, Maryland.

Searching Underwater

Amazingly, detection dogs can sniff bodies that are hidden underwater, in rivers, lakes, and the sea. They work with handlers from the shore or a boat. If a dog indicates a find, police divers search the water.

CANCER DETECTION DOGS

Scientific experiments show that dogs can sometimes detect cancer in tissue samples. They think that cancerous samples may give off chemicals that the dogs can detect. Scientists hope that, in the future, specialized cancer detection dogs (also called bio detection dogs) could detect human cancers early, saving lives.

Trainee cancer detection dog Daisy sniffs a sample. She gets a reward when she sniffs a cancerous sample.

Today, many sled dogs enjoy a day at the races! These Huskies are competing in a sled race championship in northern Europe.

5 Explorers

In the nineteenth century, dogs helped to pioneer exploration of the Arctic and Antarctic, pulling sleds of equipment in the freezing conditions. In the last century, dogs were used to explore space.

EXPLORERS

Dogs have been used to pull sleds for hundreds of years by people in the Arctic, such as the Inuit. Some modern Arctic explorers still take dogs with them to pull their sleds.

Dogs in a team can be arranged in a line, in pairs, or in a fan shape.

DOG TEAMS

It takes a team of dogs to pull a sled—from six to twenty-four. The dogs wear harnesses and are attached to the sled with ropes. They can run up to 100 miles a day, but they need to consume around 10,000 calories every day to run that much!

TOP BREEDS

The Siberian and Alaskan Huskies, the Alaskan Malamute, and the Canadian Inuit are most commonly used as sled dogs.

The Alaskan Malamute has a double coat for extra warmth

Strong heart for running all day

Wide, flat paws to prevent sinking into snow

The fastest, smartest dog is the lead dog. The biggest and strongest run at the back and are called wheel dogs.

MUSHERS

The human handler who controls a dog team is called a musher. He or she runs with the sled, or rides on the sled, and shouts commands to make the dogs start, stop, speed up, slow down, and turn left and right.

MUSHING COMMANDS

+ **Let's go / all right / hike:** start running

+ **Easy:** slow down

+ **Gee:** turn right

+ **Haw:** turn left

+ **Come gee:** turn 180 degrees right

+ **Come haw:** turn 180 degrees left

+ **Whoa:** stop

ANTARCTIC EXPLORERS

The explorers who first ventured into the Antarctic continent took dogs with them. One was the Norwegian explorer, Roald Amundsen. He was an expert in dogsled travel and, in 1911, dogs helped his team to become the first people ever to reach the South Pole.

Sled dogs sleep in the snow, with their noses under their tails to keep warm.

The Story of Balto

In 1925, an outbreak of a deadly illness called diphtheria affected many children in a remote town in Alaska. Medicine was in a faraway town, and could be fetched only by a relay of dogsleds. Lead dog for the last leg of the journey was Balto. With the musher blinded by a howling blizzard, Balto found his own way, and became famous.

SPACE DOGS

In the early days of space exploration, in the 1950s and 1960s, dogs were among many animals launched in spacecrafts. The dogs were monitored to see what would happen to them, so that scientists could get an idea of what could happen to humans during a spaceflight.

THE HAZARDS OF SPACEFLIGHT FOR DOGS

+ Very high forces during liftoff and re-entry
+ Overheating in the spacecraft
+ Danger of rocket explosion
+ Danger of returning into the atmosphere and landing
+ Running out of oxygen

Laika

A dog called Laika was the first living creature to orbit Earth, and the most famous space dog of all. She flew on the Soviet Union's spacecraft *Sputnik 2* in 1957.

Laika was strapped into a padded compartment of Sputnik. She had an oxygen supply, and water and food.

GLOSSARY

air scenting
When dogs identify a particular scent by sniffing it in the air.

bark and hold
A police dog barks at a suspect to make him or her stay still.

bio-detection dogs
Dogs that are trained to detect cancer in human tissue.

bite and hold
A police dog bites a suspect and does not let go until its handler tells it to do so.

combat dogs
These dogs assist the military, often sniffing out bombs and weapons in combat zones.

firearms support dogs
Dogs trained to work with the police to help tackle armed suspects or criminals.

guide dogs
Also called Seeing Eye dogs, they help blind or visually impaired people get around safely.

handler
A person who works with highly trained dogs. Some train the dog they work with, others handle dogs that are already trained.

hearing dogs
Dogs that are trained to alert their hearing-impaired owners to important sounds.

medical alert dogs
These dogs recognize and alert their owners when the owners' condition becomes dangerous.

mobility assistance dogs
Dogs that help people with physical disabilities live normal lives.

musher

The human handler who controls a dog sled team.

passive search

In a public place, dogs sniff people as they walk by for illegal substances such as drugs or explosives.

proactive search

A search that targets a particular place, person, or piece of luggage, because officials suspect illegal substances are present there.

puppy raiser

Someone who takes care of a specially bred puppy, giving it general training until it is ready for specialized training to become an assistance dog.

search-and-rescue, or SAR, dogs

Dogs trained to find victims of natural disasters, or terrorist attacks, people who are lost or injured in the wilderness, or missing people.

tracking

When dogs follow a suspect's path over a large area of different types of terrain.

trailing

When dogs use a combination of scenting and tracking to hunt down a suspect.

INDEX

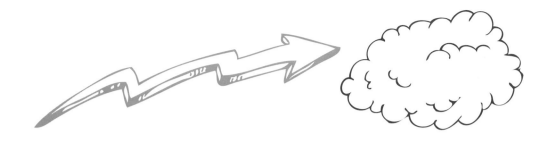

PICTURE CREDITS

A = Alamy, AP = Associated Press, C = Corbis, CO = Congohounds, G = Getty Images, HH = Hounds for Heroes, ISP = iStockphoto.com, LFRS = Leicestershire Fire and Rescue Service, MDD = Medical Detection Dogs, PA = Press Association, RF = Rex Features, R = Reuters, SPL = Science Photo Library, SDF = Search Dog Foundation, S = Shutterstock, W&D = Wood&Douglas

Front cover: G/© Scott Olson; 6 G/© AFP/Raul Arboleda; 7 AP/© Summit Daily/Mark Fox; 8-9 A/©Tony French; 10 SDF; 11 S/© Eric Isselée; 12 SDF/© UN; 13 R/© Jason Lee; 14 W&D; 15 LFRS; 16 S/© Jim Parkin; 17 G/© AFP/Gabriel Bouys; 19 A/© Ashley Cooper; 20-21 A/© Patrick Forget; 22 S/© Natali Glado; 22 A/© Yannick Luthy; 24 A/© Tony French; 25 S/© Eric Isselée; 26-27 A/© flab lstr; 27 AP/© Jon Super; 28 AP; 29 ISP/© Global P; 30-31 AP/© Jon Super; 32-33 G/© AFP/Facundo Arrizabalaga; 34 A/© Peter Casolino; 35 A/© Nancy Greifenhagen; 36 A/© Ros Drinkwater; 37 RF/© West Coast Surfer/Mood Board; 38 A/© US Marines Photo; 39 A/© ZUMA Wire Service; 40 A/© Myrleen Pearson; 41 S/© steamrollerblues; 42 AP/© Society for the Prevention of Cruelty to Animals, Los Angeles; 43 AP/© Damian Dovarganes; 44-45 C/© Markus Altmann; 46 G/© Altrendo Images; 47 G/© Spencer Grant; 48 G/© Altrendo Images; 49 S/© Eric Isselée; 50 A/© William Mullins; 51 C/© Richard Baker; 52 S/© Steve Shoup; 53 S/© Erik Lam; 54 C/© LA *Daily News*/Hans Gutknecht; 55 HH; 56-57 A/© ZUMA Wire Service; 58 S/© Y-tea; 59/S© Erik Lam; 60-61 G/© John Moore; 62 A/© Arco Images; 63 A/© Jack Sullivan; 64 G/© Gallo Images; 65 A/© Mirrorpix; 66 G/© John Moore; 67 G/© Bill Pugliano; 69 PA/© John Stillwell; 70-71 C/© Bryan Denton; 72 A/© Vario Images; 73 A/© Shout; 74 S/© Margo Harrison; 75 G/© Tim Rue; 76 C/© Radius Images; 77 SPL/© David Scharf; 78 A/© Farlap; 79 G/© Science PR; 80 S/© Erik Lam; 81 CO; 82 G/© Greg Fiume; 83 MDD; 84-85 G/© Tomas Hudcovic; 86 A/© Imagebroker; 87 S/© Jagodka; 88 A/© Robert McGouey; 89 G/© Sylvain Grandadam; 90-91 G/© Tass.